All The Tiny Anchors

All The Tiny Anchors

*A story in poems by
Sarah Thursday*

ISBN-13: 978-0692231067
ISBN-10: 0692231064

Cover art by the talented *Esmeralda Villalobos*

Gratitude
My editor: *Nancy Lynée Woo*

Without the support, feedback, and guidance from the
following people, this book would not exist:
*Alyssandra Nighswonger, Danielle Mitchell, Mickie Lynn,
Karlee and Bobby Cuff, Tina Matuckniak, JL Martindale,
my poetry parents: Ricki Mandeville & Murray Thomas,
Ann Brantingham, Renae Skarin, Denise Koehler, and my
mom, Annie Freewriter.*

Nine poems in this collection can also be heard on
Anchors, a 12 track recording by BlackSheep Music
Productions. Listen to sample tracks for free on
SoundCloud.com/SarahThursday.

For the love that had to leave
to pull the poems from my heart

Table of Contents

Part One: Swim

Part Two: Sail

Part Three: Sink

Part Four: Surface

Part 1: Swim

Plump Tomatoes

These are the kinds of poems
they want us to write,
about black-red birds and the sky
and the plumpness of tomatoes
soft against your tongue,
how it relates to our humanity
and our connection to the eternal.

But I don't relate to birds
and tomatoes (though I
will eat them endlessly)
do not keep me up at night.
When I am forced to flatten
the pages of my journal,
it's the calluses on his fingers
how I want to scrape them
scratch his dead skin off
until he forgets me,
but he has already
forgotten me.

How to Lose 25 Pounds Without Dieting, Pills, or Exercise

1. Open a Christmas card from a long lost love who found you on the Internet, not on Facebook, especially if that long lost love broke your heart when you were young enough to idealize the heartache and especially if that card was also an apology.

2. Obsess about the millions of possible reasons he sent that card the old fashioned way with stamp and pen after fourteen years of not-speaking-to-you-again, especially if there is no phone number or email included, just a return address.

3. Let him back into your well-worn heart without real answers, let him apologize again and again, but let him be unexplained and so much kinder and so much softer in the eyes.

4. Lose a lot of sleep buzzing constant with the weight you attach to his every syllable, every familiar gesture laced to his new grown-man charm, especially lose sleep waiting weeks in between the excuses you both invent to relive your lost connection.

5. Dive in very deep the moment he kisses you, do not look up, do not hold on to anything from the surface, keep pushing forward and down, let the pressure crush you, let him have every last ounce of oxygen.

6. Remain only in the present, minute to minute, live like you must love him for the lifetime you've lost, and never try to add up those years in between or account for his lack of details, live for the now reality of your skin and sweat and breath.

7. Surrender all your doubts and lay them unquestioning at his feet, do not see it coming, do not brace yourself, do not know you should have known, do not have any assurance but his hands through your hair, and do not ever regret it.

I Buried You

I buried you—
when you left
it was supposed to be for good

I dug your grave,
I mourned you for two years
Your death was crushing
but I had your funeral
I said my goodbyes

It was final,
or so I thought until the mail came
Your name on the envelope
it gripped my breath
to see your grave broken

You were shiny at my door
all flesh and bone,
not decayed

You watered the dust
and grew flowers
of apologies and regret
Dead hopes, dead dreams
all singing sun bright

Who wouldn't be sprung—
Who wouldn't feel
miraculous intervention
and long for faith
in redemption
in divinity

I buried you
I dug your grave

You were never supposed
to be standing
here at my door

Time Traveler

I step through lengths of years like ladder rungs,
step through untied moments like molecules
inside cells.
        Our time never set out
like fine china but slinky-flung down dark
stairwells. On that first night, after fourteen
years like a long locked closet opened fast,
decades fell out of my heart at the sound
of your voice.
        Your lean arms felt unfamiliar
around my hesitant skin until I reached
your hands, ending at your familiar
finger tips. I saw a bearded man
now in your college boy clothes. I was
uneasy until the softness in your eyes
settled me.
        We sat in the car dealership as
parallel souls, they made assumptions like I
made assumptions about a grown man and
woman doing practical things like Saturday
night car shopping. Just like at twenty-two
we were never lovers, but we wandered grocery
stores at midnight like intimate allies.
        As dumb college kids,
I refused to admit how much it mattered
that you only wanted to be friends. I could
never explain to the grocery store clerks
how your angry departure broke me.

I said yes when you asked
if I wanted to see you again, I said yes when
you asked to hug me again when we said
goodnight. I told you as time folded from
nineteen ninety-seven to two thousand
twelve, it was never me who ever
wanted us to end.

You reached into time,
pulled me out of the unknown to your
present tense. It took only that instant to feel
again the warmth of walking at midnight
alongside you, to feel rested in the comfort
of your voice.

I heard it loud in my head,
I loved you before and again in that exact
and specific minute. It spoke its truth.
I could and cannot now deny it.

To Agree Philosophically

It's not enough that
we have a million things in common
that we can talk for hours
about our favorite bands
and Miyazaki movies like art

It's not enough that
we agree philosophically
on religion and God
and an unknown purpose
that I respect your convictions
even if they seem ridiculous

It's not enough that
I can be myself with you
a girl-child at 37
sullen or cynical
giddy and intentional

That I get you
when you see things
no one else does
when your voice drops low
I know what that means

It's not enough that
we are nostalgic and sentimental
that we are adventurous
in the mundane things
that I just don't want to go yet
that I feel at home with you

It's not enough that
I have all the want in the world
when you don't say
when you don't show
what you want from me

Sea to Our Memory

The park was underwater
duck pond overflowing
covering sand, filling the playground
swings hanging above the surface
jutting out, half a seesaw
park benches seats for fishes
islands of picnic tables
the silence keeping a secret
all under a midnight sky

We had returned here to find it
that wooden playground ship
with splintering planks
thick rope nets and ladders
two levels of decks
for children with pirate dreams
hold the helm, storm the seas

We'd only ever come in darkness
back when as city college kids
smoking clove cigarettes
drinking wine from plastic bottles
we'd climb the top deck
and pretend not to be adults
shared this place with no one
at midnight it all belonged to us
the grass slopes and trees
the baseball diamond and swings

But it was that ship
where you first sunk me
in the dark night silence
casting those tiny anchors
with each secret hour we stole
we'd both been drifting
lost in the same current
exactly how I loved you
made sense to no one else
in our private world
of pirate seas

We'd come back to find it gone
replaced by modern safety
hardly resembled a ship at all
bright reds, blues, and greens
with a plastic coated helm
no planks or splinters
no hard knot ropes
it sat open and exposed
holding the secrets of no one

Maybe the pond remembered
rebelling over its banks, slinking out
covering sidewalks
swelling at lampposts
bringing sea to our memory
swallowing the newness
in the wet heavy silence

We never told anyone

We Can't Be Friends

Because I can't pretend
it doesn't matter
when you don't call
Because if you had a date
I could not pretend
I wouldn't feel a thing
We can't be friends
because I can't pretend
I don't hold my breath
each time the phone rings,
and my heart doesn't race
when I see your name
displayed on my screen
I can't pretend
I've never saved your messages
just to hear your voice
over and over
We can't be friends
because I can't say
it doesn't matter
if your skin grazes mine,
or the distance between us
feels like a million miles
I can't pretend
you don't saturate my thoughts
I can't lie and say
I'm not always guessing,
not wishing, not speculating

I can't pretend
we can just be friends
when I'm always hoping
it will mean something more

While I Was Waiting

In the time of unknowing
I existed in two realities,
the truth of your presence
and the truth of your absence.
I held my breath for weeks
at a time in between possibilities.
You'd stand in your doorway
and nothing else made sense.
Your proximity untied me as I
pulled your voice on like a sweater.
I knew nothing else of comfort.

I didn't know your surround,
your coarse cheek on soft lips.
I'd never known more than
wandering nights and endless hours,
how I'd loved you distantly still
past years and unspoken injuries.
You'd say good night, see you soon,
then the days stretched to weeks.
You refused to explain it,
why you'd returned this way.

I tried not to wait for you,
not to lay my head on your block.
I was trying to be savvy
keep all my options open,
fix my hair, put on a dress, get out
and smile at boys who weren't you.

Not wait for phone calls or texts,
not count the minutes of silence,
not guess at your game
I wasn't playing.

Until at a movie, we'd sit close,
arms and elbows connecting.
The electricity circulated
from my heart to my shoulders,
through my skin across yours
and into your muscles, your bones.
I felt it returning in full heartbeats,
one-two, one-two, one-two.
I could count the pulse that said
what your words would not.

Years before, you'd turned me down,
be friends now, be a friend who
buys me fancy dinners, stays out
until three a.m., sits close to me
on the sofa under a blanket.
Watch TV while I lean
my knee against your knee,
while you lean without saying
anything at all.

Lose Me

I hope you lose me.
I hope someone else
takes the shot you're missing.
I hope you regret it—
the distance you keep.
I hope someone else
fills the space in my heart.
I hope it's obvious.
I hope you know
you lost this lottery ticket.
I hope someone else
knows exactly how lucky he'll be.
I hope you lose me.
I hope you feel
a hole left in your heart.
I hope someone else
learns the secrets I keep.
I hope it's painful.
I hope my memory makes
you ache for years to come.
I hope it's easy.
I hope someone else
loves me like you won't.
I hope you lose me.

The Silence of Trains

*"You fall in love
 with someone who knows
the same silence as you"
-Daniel McGinn*

I fell in love with the man
who knew the same silence—
the silence of trains up close
in roaring motion, the strength
is deafening, a lulling voice
Its constancy feels like comfort

I loved the man who knew
the silence of city lights
from hilltops at midnight
The stars blushing down
at Los Angeles sprawled out
limbs open wide

The silence of public spaces
after dark, after closing,
after all other souls
are empty from it

I fell in love with the man
whose tongue filled
with paper and sand,
whose throat I saw dancing,
telling secrets, whose hands—
those hands said things
out loud for the first time

I'd been listening for years
Hear it? The silence, it swallows me

Slow Car Crashing

Climbed in without a seatbelt
winding mountain road
at ninety miles an hour
I know I am destined
to lie in the valley below
over the edge
in slow motion
the view
from here
is breath taking
in so many ways

Part 2: Sail

Honey

The first time you kissed me
I should have seen it coming
You were animal-starved
pawing hungry at my hips

You were hurricane-tongued
bracing me against your mouth
I pulled up fierce to match you
claw for claw around your neck

I could not hear us breathing
deafened by your torrent eyes
I did not recognize the beast
devouring my skin like victory

I wasn't your prey or your prize
bound to be death-squandered
I had waited beyond time for you
to lay yourself down at my feet

I had hoped for honey sweet
and slow to drench my lips
with tenderness. But I—
I should have known

Kissed Me Short

The second time you kissed me,
I knew I could have it.
You stood in your doorway,
soft smile and gleaming eyes.
You kissed me short
and familiar, lips less hungry,
more like, this is just
how we say hello.
Its ordinariness was thrilling.
You took me on a real date
and our hands hardly parted.
I could do it anytime now,
kiss you in the car, kiss you
in the gallery, kiss you on
impulse, like a swig of wine.
I could kiss you while we waited
for our table, hold your hand
across it, I could do that now
after seventeen years of not.
Even walking in daylight streets,
our hands clasped felt settled,
my fingers meant to lace yours.
I loved our normality
as much as our passion.
I could not yet tell you
that I loved you
and had for way too long,

but I could lean, toes up,
and press against you.
Leaping in surrender, I could
kiss you now for no reason.

Sharon as Segue

We had a talk after our first real date
I used Sharon Olds's *Gold Cell* as segue
poems of damage and fracture
told like a spy from war.
I needed you to know
enough to understand
enough to get why.
Before I shed my clothes
I had to untie those secrets
to lay them out across our laps.
Feet up on the coffee table
I had to look away as I always do
and tell you
how damaged I was
how broken my heart had been
before I ever saw it coming.
How it wouldn't be personal
how it wouldn't be about you
how I carried this weight all my life
how I didn't know if I could rest it.
You sat stone quiet
arm across my shoulders
you kissed my hair
locking your knees under mine.

My Own Body's Memory

There was no pretense, no
romantic dinner by candlelight
no soft, swaying music, just

New Order songs by video.
I was single minded, hungry—
my car couldn't drive faster.

The small talk was short, words
flung off as fast as clothes.
I had dreamt this moment

with you revised a hundred times
—all pale comparisons, roads
undriven, colors unimagined.

We stumbled across in unison
under the TV's mirrored light.
Pieces puzzled themselves

by the lick of your voice
using words like clouds on
my bare body, surrendered.

I'd add or delete nothing
I envied no one but
my own body's memory.

June, Which Returns to Me

I am weighted before it arrives.
June. The first of everything
From a seventeen year beginning,
the fourteen-year silence unfolded.

You wondered why I needed
to catch my breath. Even now.
In the span of it, you became
everything in my entire
thirty-seven year old life.

All those first moments sprung
up and around those days.
Our first hunger consumed. Our
first undressing, first devouring,

first skin matched hand to hand,
knee for knee, and mouth. Even
the vacant moments were a constant
discovering. Your ceiling rained
around us, but I forgot to be afraid.

You led the migration of how
Sharon described her old self
moving from one center to another.
In the breath of thirty days I

began the path of unknowing
what I feared of surrender,
unknowing where I would not go.
I followed you promising, I
followed you past museums and

into twin sheets after twelve a.m.
In June, you confessed, as a
Catholic child would, as I told you
my ancient secrets. I stood

heart-naked, and skin-
naked, and soul-naked.
It was one of many months set
in many years, it arrived here
on your faux suede couch

while I drank wine coolers
and played your video games.
You started it, in June, which
returned seventeen years late.

Summer Drunk

It's the heat, it reeks of his smell
reminds me of the place under his collar
and edges of his long sleeves.

How the air was too thick for sleeping
how I was constantly intoxicated
with the hum of his voice.

I lay in the green sun reading
his books, breathing his fingerprints
heartbeats between text replies

The blue sky kissed my shoulders
and thighs, grass ceilings always
bracing my body from ascension.

How I existed in the space
before you with me and without was
sleepwalking and summer drunk.

The heat hung like a red cloud
on my back and on my heels.
Here, the earth comes back

to this place around the sun
to break my sobriety
again and again.

Last Hour of 37

Just before
midnight, I lay under
the Palms Springs sky
on silver-blue foam
in a saltwater pool
with the edge of your tongue
and curves of your long fingers
pulling me towards your
liberation of my body
from the taut strings
of the bathing suit
around my neck.

Moon That Tethered Us

It was my birthday
when the tide began to change
I felt the current shift
as you made plans for me

You signed the card "love"
and though I knew
it didn't mean you were in it
it was a towards-movement

We floated on stars in the desert
peeled us bare under a midnight sun
The moon was, as it always was
kind to us on that evening

She used her gentle breath
to uproot your tall defenses
Days of summer heat softened you
and our nights became our mornings

You bought my brand of soap
and anchored it to your shower shelf
I was no longer adrift
in that vast dark ocean

I belonged at your side
now that you tethered me here

Global Warming

Every September
seems to be hotter
than the years before.
Maybe because
all the weekends I spent
in his one-window
studio apartment
waging war against the heat
with midnight baths
and dueling fans across
our shieldless bodies
humming of sweat
and creamsicles
dripping milk and sugar
in fluorescent orange
and raspberry
refusing the day-glow sun
for our own
luminescent
atmosphere.

Daylight

Your arm hit the blinds
they swung like a pendulum
    bright
light
    bright
light
piercing my eyes you
held up your hand
to stop the sun
to shade my face
it felt just like love
so I sunk
into you
in the silence

September

you needed to hear the ocean
let the tide pull on your thoughts

the sea-black sky surrounded us
as we nested on the summer-night sand

my salty hair under your chin
we did and did not talk about it

how I'd gone to the edge but no more
how it had to be you to leap out

and you knew it, you knew always
how I'd follow but not lead

how that made it easier for you
knowing I loved you first

so I asked you in the darkness why
you left me months on edge-leaning

I searched your wind-burnt eyes
you said you were shy, you said

you wouldn't want to hurt me
like years before, you said but

your words sat like sand on my skin
so I pulled you to my mouth

how your taste, I believed
how your scent, I still trusted

The Bath and Beyond

Shelves and shelves of shampoo and body wash
with colors like a candy shop sang at you secretly.
You loved how they fought for you,
in baby blues and silver browns. Bold letters
and thick lines on smooth plastic curves
like the curves of my body you drew
in outlines in our bed. Ultimately, it was the scent
that won your purchase, unscrewing caps
the way a farmer checks teeth on the livestock at a fair.
You refused to smell like a fruit or a flower.
But if by accident you brought it home,
I'd take it for you, wash my hair with it.
I could be the one to smell like flowers and fruit.

Sunken

You were always in need of sleep
always closing your eyes
lying against me
I built myself around you
a place of safe-rest

Let those deep gut-long sighs
out into our warm space
rubbed your dark-circled eyes
when I bathed you
in my wide comfort

I pressed for your surrender
my hands on your jaw
I know your eyelids
better than your eyes
You said it was me, not it

You said it serious
so I'd believe you
but sleep is not surrender
and job-tired was your cover

Your heart-tired sunk me
under, down, below
There isn't a long enough bed
I'd never be enough rest

Breathe

It was a dream
all the space you surrounded
the minutes of breathing
the hours of inhaling you.
Always, your eyes were closed.

It didn't make sense
until I surrendered to it.
I let my body sink
naked into your atmosphere.
I kept breathing you in
until you were seeping
through my pores.

The dream was warm,
I was always shedding.
Your sweat lined me entirely
I absorbed you entirely—
and then there was stillness.

You and I reflected
a single line—
it was a work of art.
I dove in love with it
inhaling, inhaling
I loved you in silence.

I asked you to see it
but still, you had your eyes closed
Wake up, wake up quick—
but it was I who was dreaming.

Measure of My Security

You bought us a bed
That was the measure

of my security
You researched couples

with active sex lives
You read reviews

to find the best for us
You were creating space

for our life together
however small

however short
You texted to say

it hadn't yet arrived
You lost the receipt

You stopped by the store
It was arriving tomorrow

You made sure I knew
it was on its way

I have proof
You said see ya Saturday

I'd arrive at the usual time
We'd buy new sheets

We'd break it in on Saturday
I know it's true

We had a farewell
to your old mattress set

We paid our respects
We had one last time

together in the morning
before you left for work

You kissed me goodbye
in your car

I felt so lucky
I had to walk away

to my car
with my overnight bag

and leftover pizza
I loved you as you

drove away and my
heart was full

and unsuspecting

Part 3: Sink

5:38

I keep smiling while I read them. All three texts. Sitting at a Greek place with coworkers at a long table for fifteen. Middle aged women and their husbands are asking about you. They all want to meet the man who put stars under my skin. I just told them about the place we found with 30 minute lines down the block, where they create gourmet pizza to order. All of them want to try it. Three texts at once isn't like you. The waiter sets the cheese on fire and everyone is opening their mouths at the flames. I'm still burning on fumes from last Sunday when you'd kissed me full enough for days. I had felt lucky all week, lucky enough for months. I read them now. I keep smiling, but I am losing the ability to hear. My head goes underwater as our table splits like an aquarium wall, everyone else on the outside. All at once I am wishing there was a magic portal to stop time, an alarm clock for waking up, cameras to be revealed as a cruel joke played. Someone must have stolen your phone, is holding you hostage, making you text those things in English I cannot translate. I have to leave immediately. I leave my coat. I leave my purse. Leave my untouched food on the plate. I try to climb into the circuits of my phone, step through satellites, make you look me in the eyes. Make you face me when you fire that gun.

Anchor

This time it wasn't
    tiny anchors pulled
from the surface of her heart
but glacier-sized

titanic anchors
plunged into the center
and instead
    of ripping out
a chasmic hole

he cut the line
       and floated away

leaving behind the weight

Fault Line

I'm trying
to line up the edges
match the pieces—
everything before

and everything since
the day—the hour
I got your message
the moment you became fractured

all I knew
and believed until then
at that specific hour

it's been sixteen days
and the edges
between my worlds
are still surreal
like a fracture in the earth

the land draws borders
a bold line before and after

the message broke us
and I can't line up the edges
I can't pull the earth back
like an earthquake shakes

your trust in solid things
nothing can be certain
not my legs to hold me
not my feet to move me

and I've lost you—
neither there nor here
you belong nowhere
none of the pieces fit

the words the breath
the sweat the skin
the night the street

the choice the hands
the light the silence

the road was wide and open
so I drove out fast
into the end of nothing
it won't line up—
the pieces are fractured

you said "I'm broken"
but I see only my heart
scattered across miles
of edges
of fault lines

Words In Stone and Liquid

You said "I love her"
sitting cross-legged in front of me
on the side of the trail, under
that tree where we'd once kissed
like frenzied lovers. The same words
I'd held between my teeth,
circling for weeks waiting
for the space to lay them down.

I thought your words were liquid soap
in the cups of your fingers where
you washed my hair with them,
dragged them across my shoulders,
down the valley of my spine, and deftly
through the inlets of my toes.

How you said those words with your voice
seemed too easy, a well-worn sweater
pulled on in the dark. They formed
on your tongue like weighted olive
branches reaching out. Her name
was old-familiar from those books
you shoved back behind your shelf.

So I laid out my own pebbled words
neatly in rows and columns, though
they would never wash your skin,
only seep in this soil where, like
a hundred times before, I sat
across from you cross-legged.

In Your Entirety

I loved you in pieces
in parts you revealed to me
in parts you served on platters
in boxes with ribbons and bows
I memorized those angles
I devoured them all
they never added up
to the sum of the whole
and I knew this

until it all broke apart
you were scattered
into millions of possibilities
of unknowns and variables

we sat on the woodchip trail
under the hanging branches
you sat nervous
scraping skin from fingers
looked at me sadly
while you pulled the sides
of yourself into shape

then you showed me all of it
you, in your entirety
that dark, sorted side
hanging on the edges
of someone else's wife

I saw the you I loved
I saw the you I never knew
more than a decade of living
around her someday soons

you designed yourself
the tragic figure beyond repair
the little lost boy
who doesn't want to be found
who needs to be broken
and live in fragments
and secrets and sadness

needs to be the things
I have fought so hard against

and I see now
why you return to her
again and again
why we will never fit
why our edges never lined up

you in your entirety
can never love me whole

Car Accident, 14 Months Going

Everything with you was
like a car accident,
the kind someone expects

months before, but when
the point of impact arrives,
no one is ever prepared.

Seatbelts and airbags don't
stop the severity of its
suddenness or the metal

frame collapsing and crushing
through skin and bone. I can
brace my elbows to my chest

stop the outside coming in,
but the forces stay in motion
and you crush my heart

in love. You leap out just
at the edge of the overpass
leaving me descending forward

in suspension. I chose
to keep my door locked
and feel the fall, feel

the collision. I still won't take
one single moment back.

In Thrown Love

No, you don't get to have back
the pressed wood bookmark
your grandmother gave you.

You got to go from me
to her in the span of less
than twenty-four hours.

You lost nearly nothing
not a beat, not a week
without sex or belonging.

There was no gap between
my endless arms and hers.
I got a canyon ache the size

of Mars and you ruined
my Thanksgiving and
Christmas and New Year's

and left ulcers in my stomach.
Left me naked just when
it was cold enough to need

your simmer stove skin.
You left me in thrown love,
confessions half spoken

your books half read
our plans half made.
I wasn't even unhappy yet—

our routine was still eager.
You stepped off our train
without any slowing down

I was still moving out fast
over tracks you laid. (Do they
still make you feel empty?)

I Thought You Were a Gift

I keep hearing your sounds
spill out from my mouth.
Your vocal fluctuations.
Grunts and moans.
I miss them.

I miss you in the shower.
I miss your naked details.
I miss your arms and legs and mouth.
The hair on your feet,
the shave on your neck.
I thought they were a gift.
None of them belonged to me.
You stole them back without warning.

I thought you had found me,
before skin became our language.
The endless hours of sharing space
driving in my car to the park
and the cliffs by the ocean.

I kept pressing you.
I kept longing for more.
I kept calling you.
I kept asking you out.
I kept staying in your apartment
on your couch, waiting.
And you gave into me.

I miss your breath.
I miss your squinting face.
I miss your toaster oven.
I miss your grocery store.
I miss the disorganized shopping.

The inefficient arrangement
of your apartment.
I miss your couch.
I miss the mess we'd make.
Constant throwing of things on the floor.
Constant abandon.
Constant lips.
Constant contact.

I miss your TV.
I miss the enormity of it.
The lack of distance.
The division it created.

We used every space in your apartment,
except the hallway.
Our list wasn't finished.
The things we meant to try.
The things we kept discovering.
I thought you were a miracle.

But I was just a distraction.
I was never an intention.
You never intended to hurt me.
You never intended to love me.
You were just trying to lose her.
You weren't trying to find me.

Scorpio, You Are Now a Libra

November, I will soon forget
why fifteen days of you
I lived ignorant of your end
for fifteen days I was lucky
to be the girl I've never been—
       a girl belonging
on the right side passenger seat
on the poorly tiled shower ledge
in between the knobs
of your long white knuckles
for fifteen days of you
I was happy and held
the head of pride on my lap
stroking its feathered cheek

Then, November, your second half
was a guillotine as sharp as icicles
you cut my proud body from my hands
       as sudden as gunshots
as dark as drowning, held down
for ten days straight and up for one
then down again—I didn't breathe for weeks
You threw away my toothpaste so

I said I loved you for the first time
in seventeen years since I first
felt that soft leap at the sight of you
You were born the month of November so
I give it back to you, the one
who never belonged to me

Gummo (From a Dream)

I saw you on TV lastnight
tall and skinnyextra nervous
your off-set fashion
twelveyearoldface
you were talking with David Letterman
(who wouldn't listen)
you kept looking away grimacing
you mention Ulysses and Snoop Dogg
I felt like calling or driving
to your apartment and no-talking
I just wanted you to know
he was trying to be nice
maybe you knew
he didn't get you
but the likeness wasn't perfect
maybe it wasn't you
he displayed his hair and his face
you are much more socially adept
still there you were
sitting in your brownpantsuit
and redsweatervest
talking about taped bacon
I just thought you'd want to know
sometimes I see your handwriting in my stereo cabinet
sometimes I hear you standing with hands on your hips
sometimes I forget I can't drink Kool-Aid anymore

Fibers In Your Carpet

When you closed your eyes
how often did you see her
How many of the things I used
were reeking of her memories

Which books on your shelf
were ones she gave you
What corners of your room
were haunted by her ghost

You thoroughly erased
all traces of her evidence
Your frames were empty
so I poured myself in

You never spoke her name
but tucked her under your tongue
You must have held her
in the back of your drawers

Tied her in your shoelaces
hung her in your winter coat
I must have stepped across her memory
a hundred times a day

She simply called your name
and you returned to her
like black mold on walls
hidden under cheap paint

So you erased me
from the space I filled
put me in your old mattress
that went out with the trash

Am I now lost DNA
in the cracks of your couch
Am I only the ghost
in the fibers of your carpet

Hate Me For This

You're going to hate me for this
all the secrets I will reveal
You will cringe at how
I describe every inch I loved
every single foot of you

Like the shape of your bony knee
or the midnight blue of your bedsheets
and the twitch in your left eye
behind thin round glasses

You'll say it's embarrassing
how I write it all down
how I read it all out loud
how I quote you word for word

Like your long, coarse fingers
I could never grasp harder
How you entered your car
on the passenger side

I loved how we got lost in stairwells
flooded parks and abandoned zoos
You always had your hands
on my ass where I wanted them

You might stop speaking to me
or wait fourteen years to apologize
You might get angry
and call me pathetic
But for every hundred secrets you kept
I will scream a hundred truths

Like the metallic taste on your tongue
and all the shoes you kept
all the toys on your bookshelves
and your refrigerator closet
the unpatched holes in your wall
and on your ceiling
and mountains of socks to match

I didn't gasp at anything
That damn toaster oven
with trapped roaches in the glass
Piles of dirty dishes
in the bathroom sink

I never turned away
from your thousand contradictions
I loved every single detail

I have the right to my memories
like the silent after-moments
or how you danced for me
or bought expensive beer
to impress my friends

Like making Twilight drinks
or blended concoctions
with orange creamsicles
on one hundred-degree nights

The first morning I woke with you
from a sleepless night you
said my eyes were a kaleidoscope
and I kissed you
in the shadow of the jellyfish

You can't hate me for this
for loving you in words
in the only way I have left

The Commercial

I saw a commercial
that made me smile
it made me laugh
I knew you would get it
I wanted to tell you
I found it on YouTube
I copied the link
I wanted to send it
    but we aren't
those kinds of friends anymore
you aren't on my side anymore
we aren't even sharing stuff
    like inside jokes
and favorite songs
you won't answer your phone
    if I called you up
we aren't getting any closer
    we aren't even close
I can't send you emails
about stupid commercials
with absurd moments
I could be wrong
You might think nothing
    of the nuances
        of the punch line
over and over I hear it
There is no one else
    I want
        to get it

Ever (Not the Lemonhead's Song)

I'd be halfway there
so I'd just keep driving
I'd just show up
without any warning
I'd just knock on your door
and you'd have to answer it
I'd hand over those books you left
I'd give you back the CD I lost
and that stupid t-shirt
that never kept your smell
because I'd washed it
before I knew I had it
I'd give you back that shirt
now that it smells like me
but I can't ever know
what you'd say to me then
and I'd never even make it
up all those flights of stairs
or walk your long steep street
or ever even find parking
I'd never make it out of my car
before my heart would race
like an engine without oil
I'd be broken all over again
before I ever reached your door

Cathedral

I take you with me
like a chain around my wrist
I took you through security
brought you to England
and on the bus to Wales
I pushed you up my arm
with bangles clinking soft

I went to Ireland to forget
the sound of your low voice
in every hotel you wait
for me to sleep without you
under pillow-white comforters
and clouds under roads
of endless miles and miles

I change my nightshirt
I change my long pants
but I find you there
in the bottom of my shoes
I met a poet who married an artist
after years and years of not
their deep folds of white skin
stinks of my undreamt dreams

I count the days unhad
in the cracks of aging stones
in ancient Scottish castles
dissolving like dead paper
black and grey and brown

they all eat like you
knives leading forks
in sway and swoon
painting food on plates
but only in reverse
pinks follow greens
orange and tan rising up
leaving only empty white

five thousand miles
two hundred days
I can't dilute you out
filling red wine with water
flowing over the rim
I see you in the gift shop
and in the hotel shower
I leave without you
touching my own skin
brushing my own hair

I am whole without you
like a lone cathedral tower
gray stones on stones
without walls or ceilings
for centuries it stands
without congregation
or faithful believers
still, it stands without you

Gasoline-Soaked

I want to write happy love poems
I want to be that woman
    moved-on, found-again
all that empowered-and-healthy shit

I want to be clear of last-traces
be all what's-his-name and
non-affected, all rosy-cheeks,
    and puppies-and-rainbows

But I am not that woman
I am still stomach-twisted
    all can't-go-past-that-exit,
paper-to-pencil and there he is

There are clothes in my closet
still time-locked, scent-stained
They hang there being untied
(over and over)
    being thrown on his floor
(again and again)

I washed them but they won't
    shake his pressed image
I'm still clock-watching and
poem-writing, heart-tired

Still breath-bruised and scab-picking
needing to watch the blood flow
    I still can't burn that bridge
he left gasoline-soaked and ready

Part 4: Surface

Shifting Anchor

And just like that
the ocean tide   shifted

The current pulled the weight
the anchor   slid
                    slow
off her rib cage

down the sides of her hips
sinking silent
to ocean sand

Her hands were still rope-raw
chest bruised black
        and green-yellow

Then the breath began
                    again
        rise and
                fall
        rise and
                fall

Lies To Tell My Body

My bones are steel-heavy
as I walk the days with it
Pores on my skin ache
weighted by the iron-core earth
pulling me towards her
Down, she says, lie with me

My eyes can't see clear
turn skull-bound, sinking
pregnant with memory
The fibers in my muscles
weep at their loss of it
motion, forward, direction

The nuclei in my cells pull
and push against-toward
refusing to agree with you
Every day, they keep forgetting
why I can't just dial the number
or drive 23 miles northwest

My arms know the exit-curves
(like the length of your limbs)
my feet know how many steps
(like the edge of your sheets)
I don't need my eyes to guide me
my hands, they know what else

But my heart knows to stay
in my honey-thick atmosphere
Lock the windows and doors
breath it in, long breaths
circulating it, the new oxygen
Lie to my body, if need be, until
I don't need to remember why

Five A.M. Poem

I say "my ex" like
you were the only one
like there never was
another heart aching

Other boys lingered
in long years past, boys
of minor importance
other nights of passion
of honey tongues, salted skin

But really
it was only you
I loved before I loved you

Only you who meets the criteria
of broken off from me
and left scars on the side
of my pumping heart

Only one who was
but is not now, but
will always be fused
solidly in my veins

So I rename you
so I don't have to say it
or hear it
part from my mouth

Box

I'm going to get a box
big enough for all of it
Tales of the Thunderbolt Kid
and your copy of *The Homecoming*
with all the notes in the margins
(I nearly licked those words
off the edges of the book)
a collection of short stories
I never finished reading
I tried to love everything
you wanted me to like
like the album by Stars
with that song, "Ageless Beauty"
(I tried to know you in it
understand why you loved it)
Then I'll pack that t-shirt
soft grey, one of many
you probably never missed
I'll fold it so it fits
next to all your other things
I won't leave a note
I'll just seal it up tight and
write your name outside
I'll drive it to the post office
and pay the postage myself

Then the box will go and
your books with your words
the damp smell of your apartment
(I'd stretch the pages to taste you)
It will all go and if I'm brave
there won't be a return address

Westwood Boulevard (Why I Can't Go Back)

I.

because I'd have too many questions
like does her husband know
have you ever met her children
do your parents know about her
does she hate your new car
or your new 60-inch TV
does she love the extra 20 pounds
I left behind

II.

because I know exactly
how small your ass really is
how you taste in the shower
how your eyes are lost
first thing in the morning
how you loved those thin pillows
from World War II
how you bought a fat one
just for me
how I know you really meant it
at the time

III.

because I'm still counting days
they are all anniversaries
of first times, of last times
of times we drove for no reason
my calendar dates lay over
like a transparency
so it's all how-long-since
how-many-days-until-it's-been
and every case on People's Court
mentions November and Hurricane Sandy
then we're standing there on the Boulevard
you said we need to talk
find some place for dinner
we missed our movie
I could unmake plans with you all weekend
it was cold enough to wear a sweater
I can almost count the hours

IV.

because I forgot to hate you
though you really wished I would

V.

because I told everyone
with eyes or ears near these words
I spoke you out loud
I own my story—this is mine
I will love it long after your scent
is rubbed off my page

The Atmosphere I Miss

At this point, it's not him
I miss, not his back of
red-brown constellations,

but my own atmosphere
I knew naked in front
of his flat screen TV.

It's not his goose-neck car
orange and black enormity,
but the happy surrender

of the passenger seat,
not driving, not road-thinking.
Clear-minded, I miss not

making plans on Saturdays
and on Sunday mornings.
It's not his tongue,

or its softness, but
the fullness of my mouth
at its opening.

Occupy: My Mind

I am crowding it out
saturating my time with
new memories, new places

new faces, new names
no time left to regret it
no space left to miss it

I crowd it out with poetry
and the local music scene
I crowd it with conversations

we had and never had
it all gets new layers on top
compressing the old so

it has no room left to breathe
no weight left to hold me back
no sound left to fill my ears

I am crowding it out with
new plans, new inspirations
new passions, new found dreams

more me, more going
more anything I want to be
I crowd it out until there is

no more than I allow
the only space you occupy is
where I put you on the shelf

Hostage

At work a colleague says to me, "How are you?
The last time we saw you, you ran out
on dinner. We all wondered where you went,
so we held your mom hostage." He jokes,
all smiling up a storm like I'd have
an explanation for him, like I forgot my oven
was on or left my wallet at home. But
I know I've seen him since that night
at a work meeting somewhere. That was
almost exactly five months ago and
I don't bring those memories to work
with me. I don't put the train-wreck
feeling on the player at school while I
got my authoritative hands on my hips.
So I change the subject. He doesn't
know what an ass he's being. Sometimes
they just don't know.

Hate Me (It Wouldn't Be The First Time)

(you know what I didn't say
you know those bits and pieces
I still protect
you know I wouldn't go that far
you know I only ever hinted
and spoke around
the worst of it all
you know goddamn well
I never named names
or spelled them out
I never led them to the path
that leads to the *real* you
so you can keep it tucked
up and away tight
like you always wanted to
you know I never gave away
anything of value
I left you in that trap of a life
all protected
like I thought you
protected me)

Present Affirmations

I am almost ready
to be over this
I am almost ready
to see you clear
that you were never really
good enough for me
I am almost ready
to pick up the pieces
I set aside
connect those dots
to pull the curtains open
to rip off the bedsheets
flip all the light switches
call you on your bullshit
see you small
and entirely pathetic
this lost puppy
is finding a new home
so you can keep that
old bitch who returned
I will not be lying
outside your door
I am almost ready
to tell you I'm too busy
I don't have time for
this fucked up game

and I'm tossing out
all the possible scenarios
of your apology
of your seduction
of your returning
I'm done with it
I'm almost ready
I am.

Striking the Match

There are some things
you get to take credit for
like lots of new punk bands
and reviving my love of reading

Like very expensive dinners
and types of beer I can tolerate
like the most perfect birthday
and the three months that followed

For making sex safe for me
and declaring my body
in all its abundance
a glorious masterpiece

each scar an act of beauty
each curve a sensual journey
All mirrors seem a funhouse prank
after standing naked in yours

I believe I am a woman
who can make men hold still
even if you were the only one
I believed any of it for

But there are some things
you cannot take credit for
like the pounds I lost
in the anxious months I waited

and the surrender I gave to you
(that you never gave back to me)
like the love I bathed you in
(that you swam inside of)

Or my voice that awoke slow
from a ten-year sleep
the voice that pulls paper to pencil
the one you didn't want to hear

It embarrassed you
so I hushed it while
you slept in my arms
It was directly correlated to

the moment you crushed me
that my voice began to roar
I can't stop its scream-singing
telling truths, detailing memories

It spills out like wildfire
and it's growing vast
You do not get credit for
waking this particular part of me

but I will thank you for
striking the match

The Truth of My Skin

Pores in my skin once
empty are now full of black
coarse hairs. Growth once fine

and translucent, now
pushes out beyond the surface,
my body in rebellion of my mind

Cells on my left eyelid
multiply fast in an unmatched race
against the right, laying in tiny folds

along the crease, I cannot
blink them out or tuck them in
they will not let me lie about

my time on earth
There are scars on my knees
fading slow, sinking into the white

clarity of neighboring skin
They are forcing me to forget you—
to forget what—to forget where I last

held proof of it
Maybe it's time to allow age
to love wisdom more than sorrow

My skin has shed entirely ten times
and again since the last time
your breath knew it

Flourish

The possibility of birth since our death
has passed, yet— in nine months
a new life is here now, where you abandoned us.
This Thursday girl, my child, my only daughter,
has become the woman you will never know, like
you once knew
the most unlit folds of me.

I birthed her from my own black ashes and none
of the fragile skin of you. She lives in my night side,
grows in those thick shards, those tire weight pocks.
She flourishes in the white vacuum space you
sucked out from me
like a plane window under pressure cracked,
spidering—
instantly gone.

She loves the deafened stillness and
grows in my gnawing hunger, grows out
through my fingernails and the follicles
of my new hair-the softness of which
you will never know—
like you once knew the lather and rinse of it.

Phantom Photographs

Imagine our love lasting,
frames filling with photographs,
both of us with drunken grins
against replaceable backdrops—
stark red canyons under quiet blue skies,
foaming waves, a thick forest,
some coworker's barbeque.
I would look at you with savior eyes,
believing my love is army
defeating your solitude walls.
My soldiers would grow fat
on the endless milk of you,
living euphoric in your studio apartment.
I would not hear their coughing fits,
lungs choking while armies fight
to fit in this space of you.
Warriors would lay down weapons,
finding work as city employees,
while the enemy perches
on edges of hilltops,
looking down at us.
Waiting.

Love Letter No. 2: To My Inner Light

There are no more demons in your closet.
We sent them home years ago.
Love burned out the last of your fears,
so you look for more to conquer.

Behind the ears of any man are his secrets.
The soft space of hair and skull and lobe.
You press your fingers to it,
it collapses under your strength.

You will fall into the space you have emptied.
But then, you must come back here.
Return from that he-space.
Breath in the she-space where
you deserve to live.

Acknowledgements

The following poems in this collection have been
previously published as follows:

"How To Lose 25 Pounds Without Dieting, Pills, or
    Exercise" in *The Heartbreak Anthology*;
"I Buried You" in *The Camel Saloon*;
"To Agree Philosophically" in *Katzenhatz* edition of
    Bank Heavy Press;
"Plump Tomatoes", "The Silence of Trains", and
    "Sunken" in *Cadence Collective: Long Beach Poets*;
"Honey" in *Pyrokinection*;
"Sharon as Segue" in *Black, White, and Coffee* special
    edition of *Carnival Literary Magazine*;
"Summer Drunk" in *Lummox II: Place Anthology*;
"Last Hour of 37" in *One Sentence Poems*;
"Global Warming" in *The Gambler Magazine*;
"Daylight" in *First Literary Review East*;
"5:38" in *Magic Tricks, Gambling, and Las Vegas* special
    edition of *Carnival Literary Magazine*;
"Word in Stone and Liquid" and "The Truth of My Skin"
    in *East Jasmine Review*;
"Cathedral" and "Flourish" in *The Mayo Review*;
"Lies to Tell My Body" in *Storm Cycle: Best of 2013*;
"Westwood Boulevard (Why I Can't Go Back)" in *The Tic
    Toc Anthology*;
"Hostage" in *Eunonia Review*;
"Present Affirmations" in *Napalm and Novocain*

About the Author

Sarah Thursday calls Long Beach, California her home, where she advocates for local poets and poetry events in the time off from her other passion, teaching kids in elementary school. She runs a Long Beach focused poetry website called CadenceCollective.net and co-hosts a monthly reading with one of her poetry heroes, G. Murray Thomas. Recently, she has been reading and recording poetry to music with her gifted musician friends. She feels blessed to have a rich life filled with all the things she loves; music, poetry, friends, family, art, teaching, and possibilities. Find and follow her on SarahThursday.com, Facebook, or Twitter. (Photo by Mick Victor)